THE SCIENCE OF AN OIL SPILL

ANDREA WANG

Published in the United States of America by Cherry Lake Publishing
Ann Arbor, Michigan
www.cherrylakepublishing.com

Consultants: Dr. Thomas Azwell, College of Natural Resources, University of California, Berkeley;
Marla Conn, ReadAbility, Inc.
Editorial direction: Red Line Editorial
Book design and illustration: Design Lab

Photo Credits: Shutterstock Images, cover, 1; Design Lab, 6; Paul Malyugin/Shutterstock Images, 6 (oil rig); US Coast
Guard/AP Images, 7; NASA, 9; Dorling Kindersley/Thinkstock, 11; iStock/Thinkstock, 13; Hulton-Deutsch Collection/
Corbis, 15; Patrick Semansky/AP Images, 16, 23; US Fish & Wildlife Service, 21; Jae C. Hong/AP Images, 24; Dave
Martin/AP Images, 27

Library of Congress Cataloging-in-Publication Data
  Wang, Andrea, author.
    The science of an oil spill / by Andrea Wang.
       pages cm. -- (Disaster science)
    Audience: Age 11.
    Audience: Grades 4 to 6.
    Includes bibliographical references and index.
    ISBN 978-1-63137-630-6 (hardcover) -- ISBN 978-1-63137-675-7 (pbk.) -- ISBN 978-1-63137-720-4 (pdf ebook) --
ISBN 978-1-63137-765-5 (hosted ebook)
  1. Oil spills--Juvenile literature. 2. Oil spills--Environmental aspects--Juvenile literature. 3. BP Deepwater Horizon
Explosion and Oil Spill, 2010--Juvenile literature. I. Title.

  TD196.P4W36 2015
  363.738'2--dc23   2014004036

Cherry Lake Publishing would like to acknowledge the work of
The Partnership for 21st Century Skills. Please visit www.p21.org
for more information.

Printed in the United States of America
Corporate Graphics Inc.
July 2014

ABOUT THE AUTHOR

Andrea Wang was an environmental consultant before becoming a writer. She helped clean up sites
contaminated with oil and other hazardous materials. She also assessed the risk of harm to human
health and the environment from contaminated soil, water, and air.

TABLE OF CONTENTS

BLOWOUT IN THE GULF

On the evening of April 20, 2010, the waters of the Gulf of Mexico were calm. The *Deepwater Horizon* oil rig floated 40 miles (64 km) off the coast of Louisiana. The water there was almost 5,000 feet (1,524 m) deep. The rig's crew had drilled a well 18,360 feet (5,596 m) below the seafloor. Their goal was to drill into an oil **reservoir** and pump the valuable oil to the surface. The project was behind schedule and over budget. But now, it was almost finished.

UNDERGROUND PRESSURE

An oil reservoir is a layer of rock in which liquid oil fills tiny spaces. The oil is trapped in the reservoir by the weight of the rock, which creates **pressure** in the reservoir. This is called the pore pressure. Without cement and mud in the well to balance the pore pressure, oil and gas would shoot out of a well like soda out of a shaken bottle.

That night, about half of the people on the rig were relaxing or sleeping. Far below, at the bottom of the well, a battle was being fought. Mud is pumped down to the bottom of oil wells to push against the oil and gas in the reservoir. This prevents all the oil and gas from gushing out of the well too quickly. Slowing the flow of the oil and gas makes it possible for workers to safely collect them. But on this night, the weight of the mud was no match for the pressure from the oil reservoir. Oil and natural gas forced their way into the well pipe and shot up the well.

OIL RIG

OCEAN

5,000 FEET
(1,524 M)

DRILL PIPE
AND WELL

SEAFLOOR

18,360 FEET
(5,596 M)

OIL RESERVOIR

OIL RIGS

This diagram shows how an oil rig like the *Deepwater Horizon* works. Locate the oil reservoir. Think about the weight of the water and rock layers and the amount of pressure that would be created in the oil reservoir. From this diagram, what can you tell about the increased risks of well blowouts deep underwater?

Vibrations shook the *Deepwater Horizon*. **Flammable** gas flowed out of the well pipe and covered the rig. Since the gas was heavier than air, it settled on the deck like an eerie fog. All it would have needed to blow up was a single spark. Alarms blared and the power went out. Moments later, an explosion tore through the rig.

Leaks from the oil well led to huge explosions on the Deepwater Horizon.

The crew tried to activate the rig's emergency systems. One device was designed to seal the well and stop the flow of oil and gas. Another would disconnect the rig from the well. But the devices failed. Oil and gas spewed from the well pipe. The well had blown out.

More explosions ripped through the rig. Workers were injured by blasts and falling debris. They struggled to reach a boat that was tied to the rig. A total of 115 people survived. Eleven men died aboard the *Deepwater Horizon*.

That was only the beginning of the disaster. The *Deepwater Horizon* burned for two days before sinking to the bottom of the Gulf. The pipe that had connected the rig to the well broke off, and oil gushed into the ocean from the broken pipe.

An oil spill coming from a well that was located so deep underwater had never happened before. Repeated attempts to seal the well failed. Finally, 87 days after the blowout, the leak was successfully stopped.

Scientists estimate that a total of 206 million gallons (780 million L) of oil were released from the broken well. Some of the oil was recovered, but about 171 million gallons (647 million L) spilled into the Gulf of Mexico. It was the largest accidental **offshore** oil spill in the history of the world.

The oil from the Deepwater Horizon was visible from space as gray streaks and blotches in the water.

CHAPTER 2

WHAT IS OIL?

Oil that is pumped out of the ground or seafloor is called crude oil. It is formed from the remains of prehistoric plants and animals that settled on the bottoms of lakes, swamps, and oceans. Over long periods of time, **sediment** covered these remains. They were eventually buried under layers of rock. Over millions of years, the remains were exposed to heat and pressure, changing them into crude oil. Crude oil is often called **petroleum**, or simply oil.

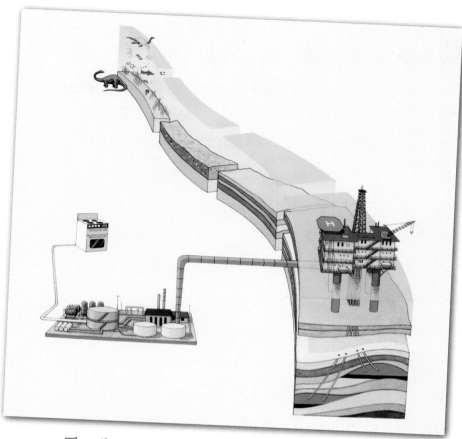

The oil we use for everyday energy needs came from organisms that lived millions of years ago.

Oil is not a single **chemical**. It is a mixture of many chemicals called **hydrocarbons**. Crude oil ranges in density from light to heavy. Some types are more viscous, or resistant to flow, than others. Oil can be black, dark brown, or even shades of red, orange, or yellow.

People in the United States use oil more than any other energy source. Americans also use more oil than any other country in the world. In 2012, the United States consumed more than 580 million gallons (2.2 billion L) of it every day. That is more than twice the amount spilled in the *Deepwater Horizon* disaster.

Crude oil is produced by nearly 100 countries. In 2012, Saudi Arabia produced the most, followed by Russia, the United States, China, and Canada. Texas, North Dakota, California, Alaska, and Oklahoma produce the most oil in the United States.

Oil reservoirs are often located far from refineries. Refineries are facilities in which crude oil is processed, or refined, and turned into petroleum products, such as gasoline for cars. Giant tanker ships carry oil across oceans. Vast pipeline networks move oil across land and water. Smaller amounts of crude oil and petroleum products are shipped on trains, trucks, and barges. Because large volumes of oil are

Oil refineries are often huge, complicated structures.

on the move every day, most oil spills occur during transportation.

An oil spill is an accidental release of oil or petroleum products into the environment. People make mistakes or mechanical equipment fails. Sometimes natural disasters can damage pipelines and storage tanks. Increased demand makes oil spills more likely.

CHAPTER 3

WHAT CAUSES AN OIL SPILL?

Oil is sometimes found in extreme locations, such as deep underwater or in cold Arctic regions. These locations, along with the chemical properties of oil, can make working with oil dangerous. Higher risks increase the chance of accidents, which can cause oil spills.

Oil forms deep underground. The deeper the reservoir is located, the greater the pore pressure. The pore pressure is predicted before and measured during drilling. Drillers respond to changes in pore pressure by

Pore pressure can push oil out of the ground with incredible force.

changing the amount and type of concrete and mud they pump into the well. If the pressure is not kept balanced, blowouts can occur. Oil wells drilled on land can also blow out. In the early days of oil drilling, these uncontrolled sprays of oil were called gushers.

Deep-sea drilling is more difficult, since the oil must be retrieved through the ocean. Oil reservoirs may lie 30,000 feet (9,144 m) below the seafloor, which can already be thousands of feet below the water's surface. At that depth, pore pressures can be incredibly high. They

Underwater blowouts are often so deep that robots must be sent down to repair the damage.

may reach greater than 10,000 pounds per square inch (69 megapascals). The risk of a blowout like the one that caused the *Deepwater Horizon* oil spill is high.

On the seafloor, drilling activities can disrupt temperatures and pressures. Large amounts of methane gas trapped in icy sediments may be released, causing the sediment around the well to become unstable and collapse. Hydrates are another hazard. These chemicals can become solid when oil is exposed to high pressure and cold temperatures. This can clog well pipes.

The chemical properties of oil also make it a dangerous substance. Crude oil and petroleum products contain volatile organic compounds (VOCs). Many of the VOCs in oil have a low flash point. The flash point is the temperature at which a substance creates enough vapor in the air that the substance can burn. Many of the VOCs found in oil have a flash point of less than 100 degrees Fahrenheit (38°C) and are considered flammable. When there is enough vapor in the air, a spark or flame can ignite it and the vapor will explode. If the oil contains a high concentration of VOCs, static electricity can cause an explosion. Explosions wreck rigs, wells, pipelines, ships, railcars, and other oil-carrying equipment. They can also injure or kill people.

Oil also contains chemicals such as sulfur and heavy metals. Over time, sulfur can damage metal in a chemical process called corrosion. Rust on iron objects is a form of corrosion. Vanadium, a heavy metal, increases the speed of corrosion. Corroded areas of pipelines, storage tanks, and ships can leak or burst.

Oil workers have developed technology to deal with these hazards and reduce the risk of oil spills. But some things, such as weather, are beyond their control. High winds, large waves, and lightning strikes from storms have all been responsible for tanker ship disasters. In 2005, Hurricanes Katrina and Rita broke pipelines and damaged storage tanks in the Gulf of Mexico region. It is believed that these hurricanes caused 11 million gallons (41.6 million L) of oil to spill.

KOMI REPUBLIC PIPELINE

One of the worst pipeline spills in history occurred in the Komi Republic in Russia. The pipeline was 30 years old and had not been well maintained. The metal was badly corroded. In 1994, parts of the pipeline collapsed. More than 29.3 million gallons (111 million L) of oil poured onto the ground.

Oil Spill Flow Rates

During the *Deepwater Horizon* disaster, responders estimated 42,000 gallons per day (159,000 L/day) were leaking into the water. Later, a scientist calculated the flow rate at about 210,000 gallons per day (795,000 L/day). This was a rough estimate. He did not know the speed of the oil leaving the well or the thickness of the **oil slick** on the water surface.

As satellite images and video of the leaking well became available, other scientists used this data to make their own calculations. Their estimates ranged from 850,000 gallons to 4.2 million gallons per day (3.2 million to 5.9 million L/day). After the well had been capped, the final, official flow rates were announced. They said 2.6 million gallons per day (9.8 million L/day) were released on the first day of the spill. The rate decreased over the next 86 days to a final rate of 2.2 million gallons per day (8.4 million L/day).

The earliest estimate was based on the area of oil on the ocean surface. It did not take into account underwater oil that never reached the surface. The final flow rates were based on new evidence: actual pressure measurements in the well just before the well was contained. Due to the *Deepwater Horizon* disaster, scientists now have a better understanding of how to measure the flow rate from underwater oil leaks.

CHAPTER 4

OIL SPILL IMPACTS

Oil spills cause harm to living things and the environment in many ways. When released into the water, oil spreads quickly and can affect a large area. Spills on land can be absorbed into soil and enter drinking water supplies. Oil can remain in the environment at dangerous levels for years. The impacts of an oil spill can be felt far from the original leak site for a long time.

Crude oil can be thick and sticky. It smothers plants and small creatures. Animals covered in oil may drown because oil prevents them from flying or swimming well.

Impacts on Gulf Birds

This diagram shows where dead seabirds were collected along the northern Gulf Coast after the *Deepwater Horizon* spill. Larger dots indicate more dead birds. Where were the most dead birds recovered? What can you tell from this data about the direction the oil from the spill traveled?

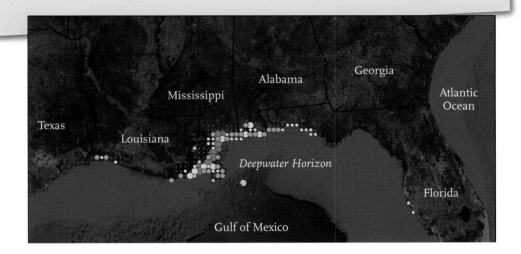

Oil is also harmful to animals in other ways. The fur of marine mammals such as sea otters helps them survive in cold water. Aquatic birds have water-repellent feathers. But fur and feathers coated with oil lose their ability to insulate and shed water. Without protection, these animals often die from the cold.

When people or animals are exposed to an oil spill, they can accidentally ingest oil. Oil is **toxic** and causes many serious health problems. Toxic compounds found in VOCs are harmful when inhaled. They may damage the brain and organs or cause cancer. Oil can also affect future generations. Fish eggs exposed to oil may not develop normally.

Even animals that do not come into direct contact with spilled oil can be affected. Zooplankton are microscopic animal organisms. In marine ecosystems such as the Gulf of Mexico, zooplankton are food for other animals. Toxic compounds from spilled oil enters the bodies of zooplankton. When other animals, such as fish and shrimp, eat the zooplankton, they absorb those compounds into their bodies. If those animals are then eaten, the compounds spread to the animal that ate them. Each time a creature eats a contaminated plant or animal, the toxic compounds are transferred.

When oil spills in bodies of water, wind and waves can

Oil from the Deepwater Horizon *spill affected marshes on the Louisiana coast.*

push the oil toward the shore. Important **habitats** such as salt marshes, mudflats, mangroves, and sandy beaches are located on shorelines. Oil can sink deep into mud and sediments and remain there for a very long time. Oil has been found in sediment 30 years after a spill. As long as the oil persists in a habitat, it continues to have negative effects on plants and animals.

Coastal wetlands such as marshes are important habitats for fish. Marshes also help purify water and guard coasts from high storm tides. Oil kills the marsh grass. Without the grasses' root systems to hold the soil

Many people in the Gulf region protested against British Petroleum (BP), the company that operated the Deepwater Horizon.

in place, tides wash away the soil and the habitat is reduced or destroyed.

The economic impacts of oil spills are enormous. After the *Deepwater Horizon* spill, fisheries and oyster grounds were closed while the wildlife was inspected. All deep-sea drilling in the Gulf and the Pacific Ocean was temporarily banned. People stopped visiting states bordering the Gulf of Mexico because of the oiled beaches and fears about air pollution. Fishermen, drilling rig workers, and people in the **tourism** industry were out of work.

Oil Spill Models

Teams of scientists work together to create computer models for oil spills. The Automated Data Inquiry for Oil Spills model estimates how the spilled oil will behave over time. These physical and chemical changes are called weathering. Another model, the General NOAA Operational Modeling Environment, predicts where oil will spread based on winds and currents.

A large database of information about wildlife in coastal areas was used to create Environmental Sensitivity Index maps. These maps show responders where wildlife species, sensitive shorelines, and public beaches are located. These tools help responders understand the extent of an oil spill, predict its behavior, and quickly come up with a plan for cleaning it up.

Oil Spill Response and Prevention

The results of an oil spill can be severe and long-lasting. The main goal of cleaning up an oil spill is to reduce damage to the environment. Booms temporarily stop oil from spreading on water. Booms are like floating fences. Containment booms can be used to surround and contain an oil slick or to block oil from reaching a sensitive area. Sorbent booms absorb oil from the water surface. And fire booms contain oil in one area so it can be burned. Once booms have contained

Workers use large booms to try to contain oil spills.

the slick, machines called skimmers collect the oil and pump it into a storage tank on a ship.

Special chemicals called dispersants are used to remove oil from the water's surface. These chemicals break the oil up into tiny droplets that can mix more easily into the water. Underwater, tiny organisms eat the droplets. This process is called biodegradation. Biodegradation breaks down oil into nontoxic compounds. Oil-eating organisms are more active in warm water than in cold water, so the rate of biodegradation depends on the water temperature where the oil spill occurred.

Wildlife affected by oil spills are also collected. Live animals are cleaned by wildlife experts, nursed back to health, and released. Because oil can last a long time in marshes and on beaches, oil spill cleanup activities can go on for years. It is important to prevent oil spills before they happen.

Old rigs, tankers, blowout preventers, pipelines, and refineries need to be kept in good shape. The United States and other countries now have many new rules to prevent oil spills. In order to get offshore drilling permits, oil companies must prove that they are following the new rules. Still, as long as people continue to use oil, there will be a risk of future oil spills.

CHEMICAL DISPERSANTS IN THE GULF

After the *Deepwater Horizon* spill, dispersants were applied to keep oil from reaching sensitive shorelines and to reduce impacts on wildlife. Scientists also believed dispersants could increase the rate of biodegradation.

Dispersants were first sprayed on the oil slick from planes and boats. Then, responders predicted that applying dispersants at the underwater leak would be more effective. The plan was experimental.

Once the plan was approved, 15,000 gallons (56,800 L) of dispersants per day were pumped down to the leaking well. This method helped prevent large oil slicks from forming at the surface. Ultimately, scientists claimed that 16 percent of the total volume of oil spilled had been dispersed. A recent study suggests that dispersants helped speed up the rate of biodegradation.

Measurements showed that bacteria helped consume 200,000 tons (181,000 metric tons) of oil and gas. Other scientists have been skeptical of these claims. More research is needed on the relationship between dispersants and biodegradation.

Top Five Worst Oil Spills

1. **Persian Gulf, 1991**
   The largest oil spill in history was caused on purpose.
   During the 1991 Gulf War, the Iraqi military destroyed
   refineries, terminals, and tanker ships in Kuwait. Up to
   336 million gallons (1.3 billion L) were spilled.

2. ***Deepwater Horizon*/Macondo Well, 2010**
   This oil spill was caused by a blowout of the Macondo well.
   The blowout led to explosions that destroyed the *Deepwater
   Horizon* oil rig. Approximately 171 million gallons
   (647 million L) were spilled.

3. **Ixtoc 1 Well, 1979**
   A blowout in this two-mile- (3 km) deep well caused a spill
   in the Bay of Campeche, Mexico. About 140 million gallons
   (530 million L) were spilled.

4. **Fergana Valley Well, 1992**
   The heavily populated Fergana Valley, an industrial and
   agricultural area in Uzbekistan, was affected by this well
   blowout. Approximately 88 million gallons (333 million L)
   of oil were spilled.

5. ***Atlantic Empress*/*Aegean Captain* tanker collision, 1979**
   A tropical storm caused these two supertankers to collide in
   the Caribbean Sea off the island of Tobago. Explosions and
   fires killed 26 sailors. About 85 million gallons (322 million L)
   of oil spilled into the sea.